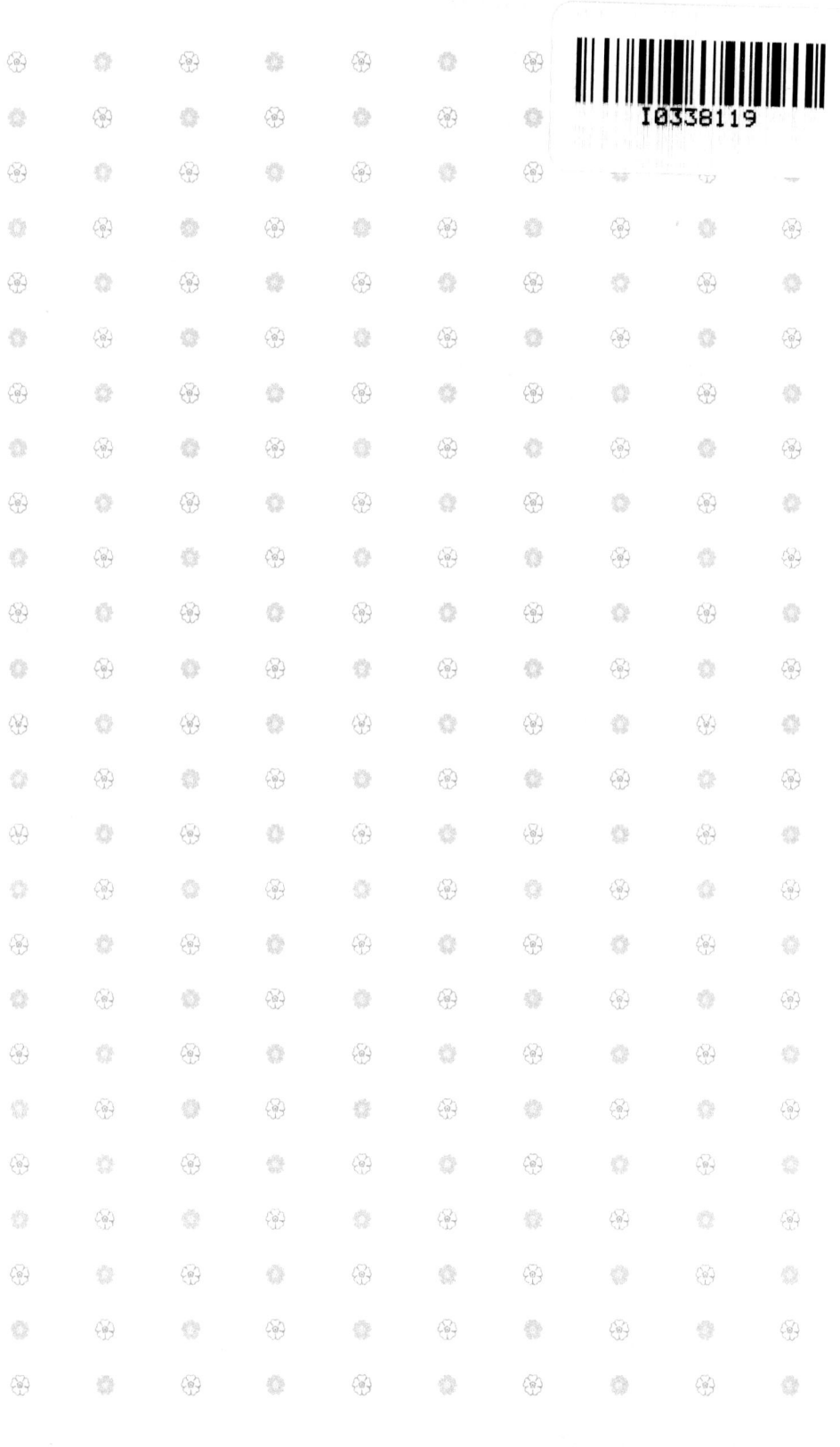

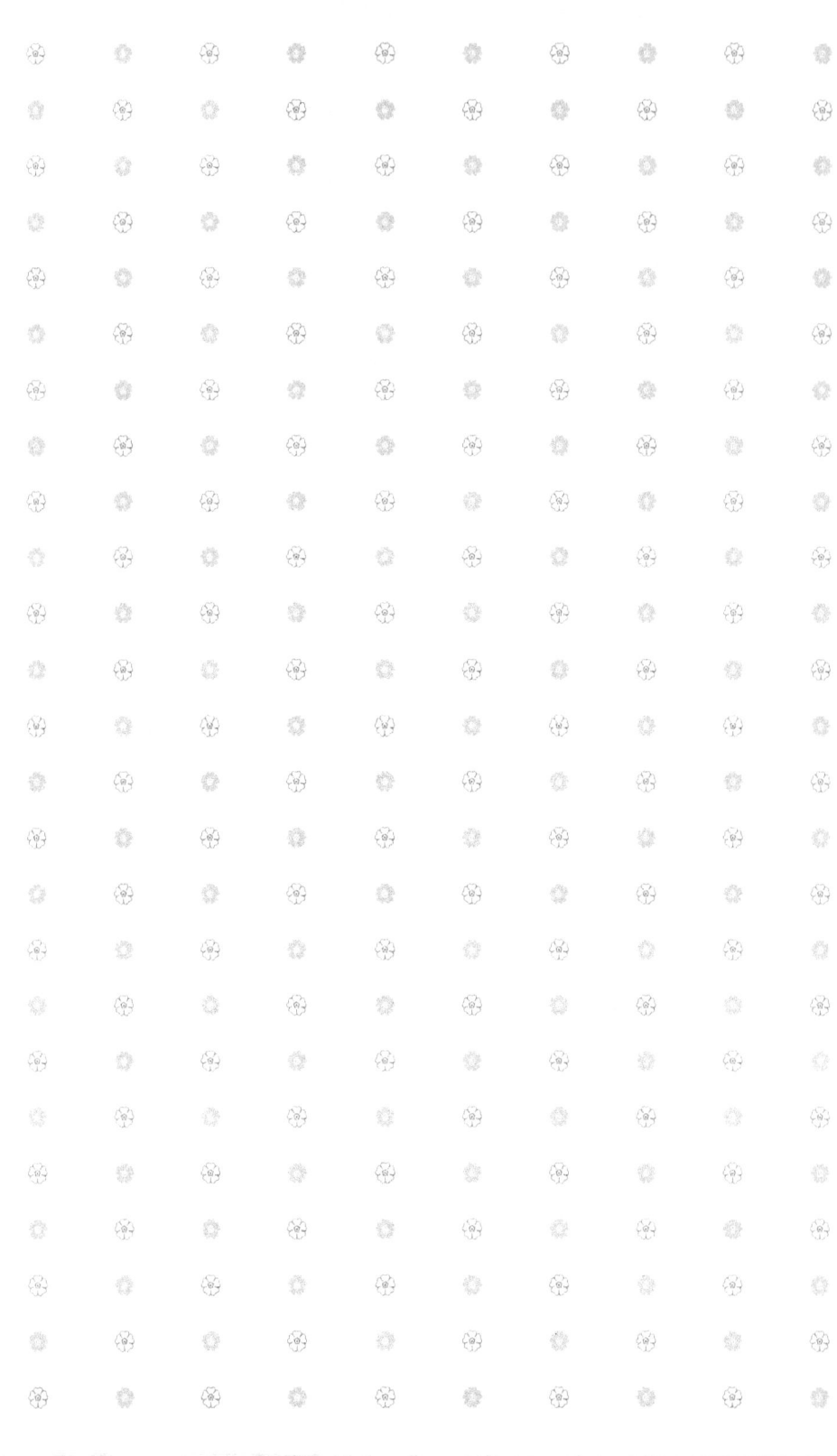

in case of emergency press

We are proud to acknowledge the Traditional Owners of country throughout Australia and to recognise their continuing connection to land, waters, and culture. We pay our respects to their Elders.

We support recognition, reconciliation, and reparation.

Bozo's Obstacle

Philip Wexler

in case of emergency press
https://icoe.com.au
Travancore, Victoria
Australia

Published by in case of emergency press 2025

Copyright © Philip Wexler 2025
All rights reserved. Without limiting the rights under copyright reserved above, no part of this publication may be reproduced, stored in or introduced into a database and retrieval system or transmitted in any form or any means (electronic, mechanical, photocopying, recording or otherwise) without the prior written permission of both the owner of copyright and the above publishers.

ISBN: 978-0-6486111-7-2

Cover design: Ward Nikriph

Acknowledgements

Leaving Marks (earlier version) in *The Medley* (Issue 8, 2023)

Dedication

To Nancy, Lucy, Mom, Jake, and Amanda

Table of Contents

I 1
    Uncertain Sleep 3
    Closer than you Think 4
    On the Home Front 6
    Let Go 7
    "I am Homeless" 9
    The Fruit Believer 10
    Where Legs May Lead 11
    The Archer 12
    Knowing How it Feels 14
    out of step 15
    Final Days 17
    Tibbett 19
    Veterans' Affairs 21
    Letting the Good Times Roll 22
    Creeps 25
    "Love is like a Faucet" 27
    World Peace 28
    Lucky Cats 29

II 31
    Aphrodite's Delight Seafood 33
    Marriage Expectations 34
    Just Now 35
    fitting in 36
    Embrace from Behind 37
    Perspectives 38
    Recollecting Ourselves 39
    Rehearsal 40
    Gas Station Billboard 41
    Directions 42

III ... 43
Bozo's Obstacle ... 45
Japanese Robot Expo ... 47
Somebody's Got to do It ... 49
Silenus ... 51
Tlaquepaque for a Spell ... 52
Taking a Gamble ... 54
Good Intentions ... 55
Strange Bedfellows ... 56
Gravity ... 57
My Mom's Sorrow ... 58
Sleight of Hand ... 61
A Trip for Breakfast ... 64

IV ... 65
Private Screening ... 67
Being Myself ... 69
My Only Memories are of Dreams ... 70
A Prayer, on Familiar Terms ... 71
Being Ready ... 72
The Phantoms ... 73
Identities ... 75
Resourcefulness ... 76
one sided ... 77
Split ... 78
I Shall not be Jaded ... 79
The Close ... 80
All Gone ... 81
The Black Bag ... 82
No, More than a Stone ... 83
So Far Gone ... 85
Human Nature ... 87
Particulate Matters ... 88
the illusion of boundaries ... 89
Beliefs ... 90
The Opposite Horizon ... 91
The Saving Grace of Turbulence ... 92
Divestiture ... 93

V **95**
    Explaining Goldfinches 97
    The Purple Cress 98
    A Perfect Heart 99
    Smoky Lavender 100
    Mistaken Identities 101
    Pigeons Preening 103
    Tree Lesson 104
    Leaving Marks 105
About the Author **109**

Bozo's Obstacle

Philip Wexler

I

Uncertain Sleep

Parched alleys zigzag.
Dogs, out of view, yelp,
and smoldering herbs saturate

the night with pungency.
I am mildly afraid,
but mostly astonished

at how I came to be
here, and my failure
to escape, until I wake

to pee, gulp replenishing
water, and comfort
my old, snoring dog

as if she is the one
having the dream.
Her eyeballs jiggle

in their sockets
when I stroke her head.
I sink into bed

and go back to the maze
of uncertain sleep,
relieved and less inquisitive.

Closer than you Think

The phone rings once.
    A bomb drops
undetonated next
    to my cereal bowl.
My life is on hold
    but won't stop.
I would be in love
    if I had the stamina,
and fall out of it
    if I had the nerve.
I reach for the phone
    but it's not worth it.
Who would want me,
    especially at this hour?
Why bother? Let the answering
    machine do its job.
A voice coaxes me
    to wake up.
To top it off, I realize
    the drip-drop, tick-tock
sounds are neither a leak
    nor a clock,
but my mucous-
    clogged snoring
at the breakfast table.
    I tell the caller
who cannot hear me, to take
    a walk and,
with the spoon
    too distant and blurry
to seize, I grab a handful

       of strawberries.
Why fret over business?
       If I haven't retired
already, I will soon.
       My head in a basket
of rolls, I fall into and out
       of sleep, unable
to tell one from the other
       nor whether the explosion
already happened
       or is about to.

On the Home Front

They drink wine
while armies spill
blood.

They snack
on saltines
and cheese

as empires
are decimated.
They can't place

the ringing
in their ears.
A passing bomber?

Don't look up now.
It might be carrying
cream pies.

The world
is a jumbo virus
hurtling through

a vast open
sore of space,
untreatable.

They celebrate
the good times
of before, yet to come,

and best of all, now,
by tossing cherry
pits at a stop sign.

Let Go

Six months already, kicked out of the navy
and let go from his job at the car wash
that morning, he sits, in a pea coat, doped
up, inside the Plexiglas bus shelter,
with the sun well into its descent.

His legs are spread wide, arms across
his knees, forming a triangular receptacle
for his pounding head, hanging down.
Dirty blonde, dreadlocked hair
obscures his stubbly, adolescent face.

He doesn't check out the buses stopping,
opening doors, drivers mistakenly expecting
him to board, but then moving on. His eyes
are open but glued to the pavement.
The only person with nerve enough, early

in the day, to share the bench with him, left
behind an empty bottle of scotch before grabbing
his own bus. Everyone stopping by since, takes
in the evidence and keeps their distance
from the sailor boy. A cold gust of wind sends

a sudden chill up his spine. He straightens
up with a jolt just as a bus pulls in.
He boards with, as ever, no destination
in mind and fumbles in his pocket
for the fare. The driver wriggles a card

out of his own pocket and slides it
into the machine. The sailor mumbles
thanks, ignores the vacant seats
and grabs onto a pole. He sways
as the bus starts moving. "You okay,

buddy?" the driver asks. "You betcha',"
he answers, letting go the pole and giving
the driver a double thumbs up
and a tremendous smile before foaming
faintly at the mouth and fainting.

"I am Homeless"

As if one couldn't tell, by looking
at her, but the words on cardboard
around her neck were an exclamation

mark to her condition. Red, scratchy-
looking blanket over her shoulders,
she hunched on a stoop outside

the public garage, a hand extended,
filthy tissue tucked under her watch
band. That day, my own isolation

made me pause, and offer her
a five-dollar bill, holding it
gingerly by a corner.

I was grateful she snatched it
without our fingers touching. Nimbly,
she folded it over twice, and stuffed it,

along with the tissue, deep
into the folds of her blanket
to nestle against a half-filled

liquor bottle. She saw me
looking, thanked me, called me
"Sir," but couldn't contain a sneer,

even as she wished me a happy day,
and that the good Lord
would bless me and keep me safe.

The Fruit Believer

It was her impassioned crusade
to reach out to her brethren,
to convert them with the word,
the genuine article, to spread
the knowledge, incontrovertible,
of lycopene in tomatoes,
flavonoids in grapes, and
procyanidins in apples, natural
wonder ingredients all, which
could ward off cancer, indigestion,
diabetes, phantom limb, and all
other ills, that led her to proselytize
on street corners, dawn to dusk,
to each and every passerby,
and at day's end, with a surplus
of advice and bags upon bags
of fruit, to hunker down
outside the Metro station,
under pouring rain, offering it all,
even bananas, provitamin A and
carotenoid-loaded, to anyone open
to warding off infirmity,
and she grew more blissful,
secure in her belief, and convinced
of her mission, the more
she trumpeted the holiness
of fruit and distributed the cure,
never neglecting to withhold
a portion for herself, all the while
attempting without great success
to curtail the intermittent coughing
brought on by the chronic emphysema
fatally seeded in her lungs.

Where Legs May Lead

He sits on a Metro platform bench,
bare legs swollen beyond imagining,
grotesque, and splotched purple, like

fungus on decaying tree stumps. His feet
are disfigured, fleshy, immense, in cork
soled sandals held together with twine.

Cracked nails curve like claws, extending
well beyond the toes. His head sinks down,
chin crumpled into clavicle, like a marionette

hanging from a nail. Approaching the up
escalator, I am winded by the sight,
and mentally break my stride, but keep

walking, pretending to be focused
on my destination. Going up,
I resist the urge to look back, unlike

the teenage couple in front of me. The boy
points, and asks the girl, "Did you see his legs?"
They laugh without restraint. I wonder

whether he hears them above the screech
of the advancing train, how he'll ever board,
where he'll go, and what he'll do.

The Archer

In blue business suit, intent on his goal,
the gray-haired gent forged ahead,
a troop of foot soldiers following.

Unobserved, we were further back,
desperate like everyone, for a way
to the Dome through the maze

of dim alleys lined with orange
and green houses. The distant shining
Dome came into and out of view.

I asked my right-hand man
who that chap was with the suit.
He leaned his face close to mine,

made sure no one was looking,
and whispered, "The Archer." Not
comprehending, I awaited details.

He mimicked the action of drawing
back and releasing a bow.
I nodded knowingly. The Archer

turned around and caught my eye.
His second in command handed him
a crossbow and arrow. He aimed

at the celestial Dome and let loose.
His men followed suit. The arrows
turned into a flock of doves. He spied

me, sought approval. I pumped
a fist in support. We pulled up the rear.
Though self-satisfied, The Archer realized

there was no room for error because
I was watching closely, waiting
for one false step, ready to fill

his shoes, take command, let loose
an aviary of my own and scale
the precarious heights to the Dome.

Knowing How it Feels

Seeing him muttering
to himself, straining
for words, deep in the Metro,

I say, "Look, I know
what you are trying
to say," and whisper

something patently
offensive. He smiles
at the perfection,

and shouts my words,
repeatedly. Commuters
scurry from his mania.

I am swept up
in the whirlwind
and board the first train

arriving, oblivious
to its destination. Silence
is momentarily restored

at the closing of the doors.
In the car, my eye catches his
and he nods approvingly.

I return the gesture.
His voice now in mine,
we rant to the trapped

crowd. Readily, they pick up
the mantra as the train
screeches in agreement.

out of step

it wasn't intention
    that spurred him
    to follow
    in the line
unblinkingly, but
    unthinking
    mimicry,
    and inertia
that kept him a zombie,
    one foot
    in front of the other
    in unwavering step.
he'd be puzzled
    when anyone veered,
    and broke rank
    willingly.
but one day, the same
    as any other,
    he felt, responded,
    differently,
jogged to the left,
    dipped to the right,
    ever so slightly.
    they noticed.
they always notice.
    he was annoyed
    by the stares,
    enraged at the whispers.
he broke loose,
    never looked back.
    the line reconnected,
    kept going, lockstep,
unperturbed.

              but for him,
                  spinning, almost
                  flying,
the guideposts were gone,
                  and the vault
                  of heaven
                      shook mightily.

Final Days

"Oriental Rug Emergency
Liquidation Sale" advertised
the sandwich board signs A-
framing the old man's torso.

His face was blistered
by days of unrelenting sun.
His shoulders ached
from waving at motorists,

and he hopped from one
sore foot to the other.
The dance and heat
were wearing him thin.

His balance on the curb
shaky, he shouted to traffic
entrenched motorists
to turn into the rug lot.

He wasn't looking
for handouts but didn't
turn down the dollar
or two offered in passing.

From a bus kiosk, a teenager,
friends in shadow, tossed him
a bottle of doctored up beer.
He smiled and downed it

in five quick gulps. In no time,
his expression soured. He flung
off the boards, and sprinted
to the Sunoco station's bathroom.

The teenager took advantage
of his absence to scrawl "Fake"
in front of "Oriental Rug",
and disappear with his friends.

Hauling the boards back over
his shoulders, the old man
was none the wiser, and paraded
in the altered signs all afternoon.

He was pleased at the sudden
good humor of the normally
cranky drivers inching
up the traffic-saturated road.

The next day he wasn't at his post,
nor the next. On the third day
a fretful, elderly woman bore the sign,
the original message restored.

The old man was in the hallway
of a cardiac unit, waiting to be
rolled into an operating room.
He blamed no one for anything.

Tibbett

Everybody is starting
to call me Tibbett. Well,

not actually starting.
It's been going on

for some time, and
for no reason. It's not

my name, never was.
I don't know anybody

named Tibbett, but
after a while I began

to answer to it. Why not?
It's simpler that way.

I can't very well correct
them anymore, for I've lost

track of my real name,
if I ever had one.

Birth certificate?
Don't make me laugh.

Mostly, I put up with it.
Still, everybody's got

their limits, and when
some kids take a time out

from their street basketball,
and call to me mockingly,

"Well, if it ain't big, bad
Tibbett," I dig up a tiny

reserve of self-respect,
and shout back,

"It's Mister Tibbett
to you punks." "Well,

if it ain't big, bad
Mr. Tibbet. How 'bout

yo autograph, dude?" One
tosses me the basketball

he's dribbling, and another
a black marker from inside

his baggy pants. I miss
the catch and pick them up

from the court laid out
in red chalk. In tiny

wavering letters, I scrawl,
"Tibbett", the ball's valve

saving me the trouble
of dotting the letter, i.

I lay the pen and ball
on the street, in front of them

like tribute and slink away.
I cup my hands over my ears

because I know they won't
stay quiet for long, and don't

want to hear their drivel,
but I only press lightly.

Veterans' Affairs

Down in the battle-encrusted streets,
another veteran grips my nose
with a garlic press, and shoves me

up against a wall. Menacingly,
he accuses my heart of beating
too loudly. I don't flinch. "You

are dead wrong, Charley," I counter.
"I am one of you." He rips the purple
heart from my chest, and flicks it

in front of an oncoming tank. I order him
to attention. He lets go of my nose
and yells back, "Screw you, Charley,"

and makes a break for it. I fire
into the air. He drops. I drop.
We crawl towards each other, reach

out to reconcile. Another veteran
jumps from the tank, one leg
landing on each of our behinds.

"Giddyup, Charleys," he urges
us on, horsewhipping our backs.
Humbled, we break into a trot.

Letting the Good Times Roll

Dining on catfish at Oceana Grill,
on Conti near Bourbon, still hung

over from the morning at the Old
Absinthe House. Picking just

the right rubber shrunken head,
one of the more tasteful choices

at the Good Times Gift Emporium.
Stumbling upon the dueling Baby

Grands in Pat O'Brien's
Piano Lounge, where I linger

for three whiskies and fuzzy music.
Holding my liquor afterwards,

and proving it to the strolling
revelers by walking backwards,

with the shrunken head between
my teeth, immune to collapse

or collision. Bargaining at Ali's
Antiques, over an ivory netsuke

of a man with a monkey on his back,
unique, Ali, tried to persuade me,

for having one cord hole instead
of two. Scoffing at the $100 price

tag and re-entering the night.
Returning half an hour later

Bozo's Obstacle

after voiding my guts
into a plastic bag I carry

for the occasion. Feeling
vindicated when Ali accepts

my final offer of $20 cash.
Stopping at Voodoo Mart

on the way back to the Footloose
Hotel for a six-pack each of canned

alligator meat and Abita Beer—
plus a box of Zombie Condoms,

and a spare plastic bag simply
because you never know. Setting

the shrunken head and netsuke
facing each other on the bed

of my dingy room and prodding
them to get acquainted. Just as

Mr. Shriveled Head finally asks
Mr. Ivory Man, "Is that a monkey

growing out of your back?"
the doorbell rings. A pair

of sluttish twins, heavily rouged
with lipstick way off course, stare me

up and down. They are from Fifi's
Escort Service, responding to a call

requesting sluttish twins for 1:30 AM,
which time it was. "Could you be

meaning my friends here on the bed?"
"Maybe so; I'm game," they answer

in unison, looking at each other,
giggling, and removing their blouses

before I'm even able to close the door
behind them. So it was to be

a fivesome. Why fight destiny?
Dizzyingly sated on beer

and alligator, but always up
for something kinky, regardless,

requesting sluttish twins for 1:30 AM,
which time it was. "Might you be looking

for my colleagues here on the bed?"
"Maybe so; I'm game," they answer

Creeps

I spied it just before daybreak,
at the edge of a door well,
under the courthouse steps.

It was crumpled up into a ball—
a tee shirt, I supposed, black, size
medium, according to the collar.

One man's garbage, I mused.
*What the hell? It's just going
to waste.* Provided it wasn't

totally ripped, or the design
too obscene, or plain pathetic,
I'd gain an extra layer of warmth,

and who was I to be picky? Good
timing. I was about to spring
for a visit to the laundromat.

No sign of who might have left it
behind. Cautiously, I tucked it
under my arm. No sooner done,

than a creep emerged from inside
the door well. He was smelly,
unkempt, (not that I should talk),

and shoved his chest against mine.
"I'll take my pillow back now,
creep," and he snatched it by an edge.

It unfurled. A yellow-highlighter sketch
of bottles of rum, women in low-cut
halter tops and dogs peeing, standard

fare for the neighborhood, flashed
before me. He scrunched it up
and retired to his dark interior,

muttering to himself, "Creep."
The sun was rising. I moseyed
back to my own secluded lair.

Damned if I'll offer him
a good deal on one of the down
pillows I filched from Saks.

"Love is like a Faucet"

He wears a blue rain poncho, and a yellow Acme Plumbing
baseball cap, and sits at a rickety table the size of a dinner plate,
in Joanne's Cafe. With a contortionist's ease, he crosses
his legs over twice, like the intertwined limbs of a tree.

Intently, he compares his Mega Millions lottery ticket with
the winning numbers on the TV overhead, and tears it
into little pieces. He shifts his eyes to the jukebox, listening
to a smoky female voice singing, "Love will make you do

things that you know is wrong" and shakes his head in accord.
Joanne herself refills his thermos halfway. He puts a little
something extra in to top it off, and drinks. Outside,
it's raining. He mouths along, "Love is like a faucet, it turns

off and on." He caps the thermos and stuffs it into his canvas
shoulder bag. Making sure to catch Joanne's eye, he leaves
a dollar bill on the table and puts on his hood. She winks.
He smiles, the one time that day. He stays dry in a bus shelter

on a bench next to an old couple, and sings, "Sometimes
when you think it's on baby, it has turned off and gone."
The couple exit briskly and opens their umbrella. The rain
lets up. He goes to the newsstand, buys a lottery ticket.

World Peace

It was a wild goose chase, I should have known from the start,
down Market, Maine, Jefferson, Fourth, Porter and Third.
With the smoke, flames, and devastation, I couldn't find my way
back to the staging zone, and settled for a mostly empty parking lot
far from the action and off the grid. The sudden quiet
gave me a wicked headache. Another lost soul offered me
a snort, on the house, but I'd been there once too often.
The stars were coming out as I struggled to assemble the 3-D
jigsaw puzzle of world peace I'd been lugging around
since the hostilities began—fifty thousand unlabeled plastic
pieces. I unscrolled the faded and waterlogged three foot
square picture I needed to recreate in space. The "answer key"
on the back was equally unreadable. Passersby couldn't resist
putting in their two cents worth but they knew no more
about world peace than me. The job was wearing me out
and, honestly, my heart wasn't all that into it. With night
upon me, I was sure to lose my way if I tried to retrace
Third, Porter, Fourth… who remembers? I left the pieces
scattered on the lot, and grabbed a bowl of potato soup
from the passing food wagon. A few blocks away, I found
myself a patch of green lawn, a rarity in those parts. I zipped
up my sleeping bag and watched the stars. Far off, I heard
the hum of grenades, rifle fire, rockets—familiar sounds
to lull me to sleep. Could it get any better than this?

Lucky Cats

With a film of clammy misery wrapped
around you all day, rain was inevitable.

It delivered while you stood transfixed in front
of the six ducks in the Chinatown storefront,

hanging by their necks. On the pink-stained sill
underneath, lucky cats, multi-colored glazed ceramic,

half-price, were bobbing their smiling, spring-
loaded heads and waving their paws. Outside,

sheltered by the awning, and bundled between
blankets piled as high as your waist, Walter,

itinerant, homeless, harmless, was the living
member of the tableau, and this by a thread.

As always, he brought you closer to yourself,
and under the gray, saturated sky, you were kin.

You gently sprinkled a few coins into his bowl.
His eyes, peering out from the layers, thanked

you. In a muffled voice he added that someday
he'd come out of it. You assured him that

you had no doubt, and went inside the store
for two lucky cats, one to gift, and one to keep.

II

Aphrodite's Delight Seafood

It was all in the way she failed
        to react to my farewell
hug in the parking lot
of the Greek restaurant,
where we shared our first meal.

I should have realized even then
        that her neither resisting
nor embracing me but dangling
        in my arms, flaccid,
like a flounder on a hook too long
out of water to put up a fight
was a foretaste of our future together.

But having doubted the likelihood
        of her paying me any mind
at all, I was enough encouraged by this
        feeble engagement to follow
up with a call, to initiate

the usual chain of events. The outcome
        of it all was my letting her
string me along for weeks. Once
        we started to drift apart, I came
to my senses and, much to her delight,
        took the lead in accelerating
the pace of our inevitable split.

Marriage Expectations

I told her not to expect it
would be like the marriage
of her friend who held the nail
while her husband hammered.

Not that I wouldn't bang
my share, putting up shelves
for her to line, and painstakingly
harvesting lentils I would plant

so she could make soup.
And I'd be grateful having her
adore the sparrows floppingly
reveling in the birdbath

I improvised from an upturned
trash can lid while I praised
the tiny blue tiles
she glued to the rim.

We'd get by just fine absent
hand-in-glove tightness
and do just fine hammering
our own respective nails...

or so we expect.

Just Now

I'd rather not know
        the details
of your inconstancy
        or how far
you will unfurl.

I'll take doubt
        over certainty,
for wondering
        at least
leaves open doors.

Forgo excuses,
        defenses. Go,
roam as you choose.
        I'll be here
should you revert.

Keep me guessing
        at your motives.
Just now
        it's as much
as I can bear.

fitting in

wild violets, purple
and white, weed-proud,
garnish my lawn,
       break the boundaries
       of local ordinance.

i brush aside complaints
of "noxious, rank vegetation"
and relish their spontaneity
       synchronized
       with spring's promise.

let the whiners lobby for the prim
and proper all they want.
it's the off kilter keeps me
       stable, nimble
       and sane.

the imperfect bed of flowers
and grass summons me
to decamp from my too
       unblemished indoor
       hibernation.

let nature seek its natural
excess, overcoming borders
and boredom
       and the threatening
       rain let loose

to further spurt weedy growth.
i will relish the windy drenching
no matter if i'm knocked down,
       for petals of reassurance
       are sure to break my fall.

Embrace from Behind

In the lobby's mirror,
    which you were unaware of,
I saw you sneaking up
    behind me, and snaking
your arms around my waist,
    but it didn't take your reflection
or your smooth bare skin,
    or the red coral bracelet
I'd given you, or to hear you say,
    "Guess who?" to tip me off.
I would know, as I always do,
    before my senses come into play,
that you are close, and closing in,
    and totally after my own heart.

Perspectives

As she withheld,
        he withdrew.
As she withstood,
        he withered.

It was the lake
        mattered to her
in their sailing, the woods
        as they hiked.

She was surprised
        he found that
surprising. But it was her
        mattered to him

the most, on water
        or land
and he was surprised
        she didn't get it.

As she chattered,
        he coped
but once she chided,
        he choked.

Recollecting Ourselves

Fog-besieged, we took
      the briefest of strolls
under the slimmest of moons
      on the promenade
of the yet unpolluted Huangpu
      River before the Pudong
skyscrapers aimed skyward
      or the squat stone
buildings of the Bund rose
      from their foundations.

Do you too, reflect
      on our failure
to have seized that instant?
      I'm not consoled
by the memory, but lament
      what I lost and lack.
Leaning on the railing, we looked
      every which way
but at each other, asking
      of ourselves not enough.

Rehearsal

On weathered steps
        overlooking
                the harbor,

she crouches,
        in long, black
                skirts, pensive.

She waits for my ship
        to come in, for
                our reconciliation,

but I approach from behind,
        wondering when
                she'll concede I'm here.

I never shipped off
        nor had the urge.
                My head hangs low.

She knows all this,
        but concentrates on the horizon.
                Once I touch

her back, she turns
        around, her face unreadable,
                and enfolds me

as if I'm just back
        from the wars,
                barely returned

with my life.
        I admit nothing
                for she wouldn't want me

to spoil the effect.
        We learn our roles
                as we go.

Gas Station Billboard

A good dozen feet long, and maybe half
as tall. A life sized, barely swim-suited

model on a pink webbed beach chair.
Her endless legs not crossed, but grazing

each other seductively. I can feel
the heaving of her overflowing chest

as she bends down to strap on a sandal,
which brand the ad is touting. A wet lock

of hair dangles over her forehead.
She wants to cringe, I know, at the bird

stains on her cheek, marring her beauty.
I am infuriated by the offense, and want

to restore her perfection. Squeegee in hand,
I scale the billboard, anticipating no thanks

for my efforts, and wishing for no more
than to lose myself in her profusion of legs.

Directions

I'm looking for you
to go arm-in-arm with me

where I'm headed or nudge
me in a different direction

but not budge from my side,
and hold me back from retracing

my steps to the solitary place
I'd given up on and quit,

to throw my lot in with you.
Blindfold and spin me

and I'll happily lead us
where you leave me pointing

when I stop. What could
better assure we both stay

on track? How better
to ensure our survival?

I am looking for you
to see us through.

III

Bozo's Obstacle

1. Discovery

I discovered it, like most everything
of consequence, by happenstance,

in a cardboard box overstuffed
with nostalgia—a local newspaper

clipping, decades old, headlined
"Junior Putters take Top Honors

in Miniature Golf Tourney". Below
was a close-up of my younger self,

third-prize winner next to the older kids
who beat me, each of us one-handedly

lofting a golden-hued plastic trophy
of a golfer in mid-swing, sized

proportionate to our standing.
Immediately, my mind flew back

not to the prize, but to the memorable
final hole, *Bozo's Obstacle*.

2. Reprieve

He was a boxy clown of plywood,
bisected by a motorized axle.

His clunky hollow legs opened
and closed with clocklike regularity,

and his splintered yellow eyes defied
me to stroke the ball through. I did.

With their prey slipping away,
Bozo's feet clopped together

dejectedly behind the wily ball.
It rolled up the bank to a circle

of fake grass, for a hole in one,
only to pop right out, followed by

a confounded mouse, who scrambled
up one of Bozo's legs. The judge,

my uncle, Sammy, kicked the ball
back in to let the record show

I would suffer no penalty
on account of a rodent's folly.

3. Vendetta

I didn't read the story straight
through but turned to page three

where it continued and I found
another photo, this one of Bozo,

clear as day, lifelike, a squiggly,
thin line hanging from his smiling,

chalky lips. It might have been
a string or noodle or wire.

Maybe even a tail, maybe
even a mouse's.

Japanese Robot Expo

On stage, archetypal robots looking as expected, march
in a precision drill, forward and back, side to side,
do knee bends, stand on one leg, and climb ladders.
In the rest of the hall, androids, uncannily lifelike,
engage in daily human activities. One, in a three-piece
suit, sits at a keyboard, repeatedly typing, "I am
an android, not a robot." Another, wearing a floral
kitchen apron, chops celery, carrots, and potatoes,
which a seemingly real teenage girl carries to a pot
of boiling water, to make soup. Framed
in a shallow boudoir setting, a cyborg looking
astonishingly like a beautiful flesh and blood woman
in a blue kimono, washes her long black hair in a pink
marble bowl. Her name tag says, "Call me Haruko!"
I fall in love with her instantly, and fear she will
electrocute herself if moisture works its way
into her circuitry. She bows and smiles
when I hand her a towel from the rack,
unintentionally obeying the sign I later see,
saying, "Give Android Towel!" Her cheeks
blush as she almost sings, in an angelic voice,
"Thank you," with a slight Japanese accent.
The crowd gradually shoves me aside for a glimpse.
Infatuated, I wander around the hall in a daze,
looking back to catch Haruko's eye. I take a break
in the driver's seat of a floodlit convertible,
set up for another show starting shortly,
and am mistaken for a cast member. On the hood,
a digital sign instructs, "Ask Android Question!"
A couple encourages their little girl, who asks
my name, my age, and whether I can drive.

I answer easily in a choppy monotone. I falter,
though, when a sneering young man wants to know
the speed limit in Croatia and why I didn't shave
this morning. I begin stuttering and cannot stop.
I see concern in people's faces. Technicians
in white lab coats carrying various and sundry
implements, hurry over. One handcuffs my hands
behind my back. The other secures my chin
with one hand and positions a cordless drill
over my head. In the car's rearview mirror, I catch
sight of Haruko, arms outstretched, yellow
butterfly patterned sleeves flapping, and desperate
to keep upright in wooden clogs as she is unsteadily
      running, running while I resort to helplessly mumbling,
          "Quickly, quickly."

Somebody's Got to do It

The new soccer stadium
was getting its finishing touches

which, for an army of volunteers,
meant finishing flushes.

Their job—to give the plumbing
system a run for its money

by means of the synchronized
flushing of 100 toilets and urinals.

The protocol was to press
down firmly and without hesitation,

with thumb and forefinger only,
in a single movement, and release

at the bottom of the stroke
in an cqually unflinching manner.

A precisely timed series of beeps
over the intercom would serve

as the signals to flush, once
a minute, 15 times. The volunteers

were asked not to relieve
themselves, except for emergencies,

during the flushing period,
although they were allowed to

do so in the thirty-minute break
after phase one, and before

the flushes were repeated
for another 15 minutes.

After the event, the crew
was congratulated and debriefed.

The flush went off without a hitch.
Coffee and cake were served.

Everyone was invited to help
themselves to a free *Pee Shirt*,

or so the box was labelled.
On the back of each was a photo

of the stadium emblazoned
with the team's name,

and on the front, the stainless
steel toilet bowl handle.

Watery blue letters underneath it
spelled out, *Flushed with Pride.*

Bozo's Obstacle

Silenus

The only one you hear tell about is the kid.
How he, Dionysus I mean, ever became boss
is an eternal puzzle. Alright, maybe he holds
his booze better, is sharper at bewitching
the ladies and can lead them and louts
like me around by his pinkie, but this doesn't
make him more deserving of praise than me,
his ill-used tutor, who taught him all he knows.

His revelries they call ecstatic wine worship.
Pathetic cultism if you ask me. Alright,
I join in now and then myself. But how
did he come to be a god anyway, he
with a mortal mother yet? Me, they label
a drunken, bloated buffoon, though
I have a good thirty years on him,
and consume not a smidgen in comparison.

Where's the respect that comes with age
and dignity? They think I am dependent
on my mule or the satyrs for support.
Not a bit, I can assure you. I only lean
on them as dear companions. I confess
I may stumble on occasion, but am, by far,
more stable than they imagine, plus
I can prophesy. There's a handy talent.

Ah, Dionysus, my carousing student,
it could have been me that was heralded
and acclaimed, but I was generous to you
with the gift of wine. Don't speak to me
of predestination and gratitude. Save
your smug condescension. Here, my boy,
give me a hug for old times' sake,
before I buckle. I can't hold it like I used to.

Tlaquepaque for a Spell

The expatriate Mexican banker
flew back from the States,

for a quick visit to his home
town with the click-clack name,

overgrown with crafts and tourists,
moments from Guadalajara,

to pay regards to his brother, Oscar,
wheelchair bound and fading,

and his loving wife, Lola, ever
the knockout. They dined

at El Patio restaurant. He tipped,
to embarrassing excess the mariachi

for one old time song after another.
The bouncy music, and the Patron

silver tequila, comforted Oscar,
eyes closed in reverie. Lola,

stirred by like memories, dabbed
her own, smearing them, and blew

her nose with coarse paper napkins.
She latched onto her husband's hands,

folded neatly on his lifeless lap,
but couldn't divert her eyes for long

from her brother-in-law's insistent leer.
The old standard, *El Mariachi Loco*,

a favorite of theirs, about the crazy
mariachi who wanted to dance,

was crazy enough to set them all
to laughing with abandon.

So neighboring tables could see,
the banker held up a tight roll

of American dollars, secured
by a red rubber band

and handed it to Lola for medical
emergencies he said, with a wink.

This made her cry again. He looked
wistfully at his brother, now

in a hopeless daze, as the band
took a break at the bar. He downed

his tequila, and hugged them both,
with an extra posterior squeeze for Lola.

She blew kisses at him
as he hurried into the idling

white limousine, to take him
to his private jet for a midnight

meeting on Wall Street, and
pre-sunrise clubbing uptown.

Taking a Gamble

He would rush his enemies
with bloodcurdling cries,

shed his armor and taunt
them to shoot at his bare chest.

He dodged every projectile,
and performed little victory

dances between attacks.
The enemy thought him insane,

and he would be the last
to deny it. Even his comrades

in arms kept their distance
when he was on the warpath.

He came through it all
unscathed, decorated, still

crazy, but not strident,
and trying to make sense

of civilian life. Outside
the convenience store,

he was rubbing numbers off
a losing lotto ticket

as a sniper's bullet cleanly
pierced his neck from behind.

Good Intentions

On the day after Christmas
five years ago on trash pickup
and recycling Friday,
on the smidgen of lawn,
in front of the townhouse,
a mint condition exercise
bicycle with a paper sign
on the handlebars—"Help
Yourself". Next to it
an empty cardboard box
labeled, "Harrison Treadmills".

On the following
year's post-Christmas
trash day, the treadmill,
not a mark on it, offered
"To a Worthy Home".
So it went, year after year—
rowing machine, elliptical
trainer, barbell set—prior
year acquisitions, free
to haul away, and current
year packaging to discard.
Good intentions all.

Most recently, nothing
of the sort—just the trash
cans and recycling bins,
overflowing with beer
empties. And some weeks
later, a siren, an ambulance,
a stretcher, and before long,
a sign on a stake—"For Sale".

Strange Bedfellows

It was already over a week
since my defective valve

was replaced by a pig's
and I was three times bypassed.

I'd emerged from the worst
of it and begun rehabilitation.

Stretched out on my back,
eyes closed, trying to nap,

it sounded as if my heart,
pig part and all, was in bed

beside me, beating fiercely.
Mentally, I was telling it

to slow down, take it easy,
that I would always be there

for it, and it seemed,
breathlessly, in between

what could only be
described as oinks,

to be reassuring
me of the same.

Gravity

The regulars on the group walk knew
to keep their distance from him, but

he was able to corner the incredulous
college girl, a newcomer, to explain

his convoluted computer indexing project
designed to "release the universe

of knowledge from its literal constraints".
He asked her to give him a topic,

any topic. She raised a finger to her lips
for a second's thoughtful pose

and said, "Gravity." "Okay, good, gravity,"
he repeated, like an automated customer

service agent. He went on to explain
how his algorithm could generate

"unique and unambiguous semantic facets
on gravity, heuristically optimized".

She was superficially attentive, but mentally
rolling her eyes. Did she follow his line

of reasoning? he wanted to know.
"It has merit," she conceded, "but

did you notice the dragonflies at the lake
where we stopped for lunch?" He stared

at her, confused, finally concluding,
"Gravity. That's good. I'll make a note."

He fumbled for his pen, but it fell,
and then, reaching for it, so did he.

My Mom's Sorrow

Wheezing, my asthmatic grandpa
held my hand securely, and led me

through the congestion of Sao Paulo's
hilly streets, with the reluctant permission

of my over-protective mom, who would
inherit his condition years later.

She acceded to his wish for the two of us
to spend some time together alone

that bright morning on his home turf,
before my summer holidays were up.

He let go of my hand when we reached
the tiny stamp and coin shop at the peak

of a hill. His chest rattled as he asked
me to pick out what I might like.

He conversed with the dealer in Portuguese.
I settled on a slim leather-bound album

with thick black pages and horizontal
strips of clear plastic to hold stamps,

a leather rimmed magnifying glass, and
assorted stamps of colorful Amazon parrots.

I told Grandpa I knew how to squawk
like a parrot, and he laughed abundantly

at my performance. He paid, and tipped
his hat to the dealer. I held the brown

shopping bag in one hand as he led me
by the other back through the confusion

Bozo's Obstacle

of the undulating neighborhood and into
the hotel lobby where mom waited anxiously

to repossess me. I was embarrassed
by her over-the-top hug, replicated

on Grandpa who, while winded,
was nonplussed. He told her how

delightful an excursion we had and how
well behaved I was, and began to recount

some story about when he was my age,
which I didn't have the patience

to pay any attention to. Interrupting,
I held up one of the parrot stamps

and the magnifying glass in front
of it, hoping to enlarge the bird

enormously in his eyes. I tugged
at his sleeve and, catching

his attention, started squawking
again like a parrot because I knew

it amused him so. This time it led
to a prolonged coughing fit preventing

him from resuming his reminiscence.
Uncharacteristically, Mom smacked

my cheek and settled Grandpa
into a cushy loveseat. He slid a flask

out of his pocket and took two swigs.
Once he caught his breath, he insisted

he didn't need anything else,
and certainly not the clinic Mom

was eyeing across the street. She looked
a good deal more ashen than Grandpa

whom she sat beside while clutching me
around the waist. In turn, she patted

the back of his hand and kissed my cheek,
stinging from her slap. Hoarsely, she kept

repeating to neither of us in particular,
how sorry she was, how truly sorry.

Sleight of Hand

We didn't have a chance
      to exchange
our usual annual greetings
      prior to the opening

scientific session
      where he was
introduced and welcomed
      on stage.

It pained me to see
      his right hand
with a mind
      of its own.

I hadn't noticed
      any tremor
at last year's
      conference.

But now it was
      pronounced,
and he hardly knew
      what to do

with it as he presented
      his research findings
from the lectern.
      The vibration extended

to his shoulder
      when he put his hand
in a pocket.
      Least noticeable

was clasping both hands
    together on the lectern
for stability. I studied my own,
    spread on the desk

in front of me, wondering
    if the condition
might not be contagious
    like a yawn,

but they were smugly
    at peace.
After the applause
    and the questions

and more applause, he took
    a seat, not noticing me,
at a table to my side.
    He made his hand

disappear by retracting
    it into his jacket sleeve
where it seemed finally
    under control.

He listened distractedly
    to one speaker
after another, slapping
    his good hand

on the table when it was time
    to clap. As the session
ended and everyone rose,
    he saw me and came over.

I offered my hand
    to congratulate him
on his talk. "Presto,"
    he said, extending

Bozo's Obstacle

his, in check for the time being,
    from the jacket.
I tried to act
    as if nothing

had been amiss,
    and made quite sure
the handshake
    was not too brief,

A Trip for Breakfast

Ostrich milk
        on gold
flake cereal,
        sprinkled
with glowing
        mulberries,
iridescent purple,
        drizzled
with deep subterranean
        melodies.

Dig further down
        to the rainbow's
roots, the birthplace
        of aspirations,
where the mirage
        of yellow
blends with its incarnation,
        and the purity
of sleep
        is unhindered
by the call of morning.

Pause, on the descent,
        to alert the misguided,
shoveling up
        to break the surface,
that they are abandoning
        a better place
and all that waits
        for them will be charred
toast and tepid tea.

IV

Private Screening

"Wait up, Eric," but Eric was deaf
to his little sister's pleas, hopped

on his bike, and was out of sight
before she started pedaling. Emma

had no idea where, so she took a left
and a right, and a left, and kept going,

shouting "Eric" every so often,
exhausting herself for well over an hour.

Miraculously but dejectedly,
she found her way back home,

with a flat. Eric had been there almost
the whole time, having given Emma

the boot by sprinting once around
the block. He had just concluded

watching the latest X-rated DVD
his parents starred in, which they must

have let slip by the front door on the way
to their day jobs in the morning.

He had already repeatedly viewed
one he'd found in the driveway

a few months ago so was jaded
by the whole affair. He and his sister

glared at each other. "Want to take
another bike ride?" Eric asked

with a smirk, provoking her
into rushing him. They banged

into the video device, which began
replaying the movie on their 65-inch

screen and was not responding
to Eric's desperate attempts to turn

it off and who had no luck shielding
Emma from the action by feebly

blocking a small part with his body.
As she watched, dumbfounded,

their chatting parents came in
the front door. Taking in the scene,

the adult film stars hushed up,
froze, and dropped their packages,

including two new videos
in the same vein.

Being Myself

1.

I turned around
    because I heard
someone calling,
    and it was my double,
his back to me, calling
    to someone further back
whom I could not see.
    Relieved, I kept on
following my footsteps.

2.

After too long a wait,
    the elevator arrived.
Stepping in, I saw
    my double coming out.
We grazed each other.
    He hurried across
the lobby, through the revolving
    door, and into the street,
never looking back.

3.

I stumbled upon an online video
    demonstrating hypnosis.
It was my double, asking me to look
    into his eyes. I had trouble
focusing. He told me
    I was getting sleepy,
but I was sleepy to begin with,
    just waking up from a dream
of being someone else.

My Only Memories are of Dreams

In the Roman arena at Aix-
en-Provence, I am solitary

but far from alone, the only one
not party to the ritual of holding

candles at dusk, waiting
for the performance of Delibes'

ballet, *Coppelia*, the lifelike
mechanical doll, to begin.

Wax melts and flames grow
brighter as darkness and the story

unfold. Like the character, Franz,
I am infatuated with Coppelia

but also with the candles
and the night. Orange flames

are snuffed out one by one
in puffs of smoke. Coppelia

and Franz blow kisses
to each other. I am buoyed

by tiny air currents, and follow
wherever the score leads.

I remember it as clearly
      as the dream
           I always dreamt
                of having.

A Prayer, on Familiar Terms

As the twilight of one year
nudges forward the dawn
of another, and the finish
line transforms to starting
gate, I look more ahead
than back, take heart
at the trumpet's calling.

Perhaps this time
the threshold moment
will buttress my sagging
belief and help me clear
a fresh path through
the tangled brush, with
a honed machete of hope.

How better to attain faith
than by your blessing
my conviction to act.
Forgive me again
if you would and, provided
I don't presume too much,
let's shake on it, Lord.

Being Ready

Whenever I get down
        to deciding, it's too late,
sold out, closed,
        boat already left,
we went ahead and ate
        without you, so sorry.

So I promise myself, tomorrow
        things will be different.
I'll set in to itemizing
        choices, prioritizing options,
consult maps, clocks, computer
        simulations, everything

synchronized, not waste
        a minute, make plans well
in advance for the next day,
        week, millennium, any
eventuality and, above all,
        be ready. But I forget

to set the alarm.
        I oversleep, and when
the Messiah comes
        to gather up the chosen,
I'm snoring
        deeply, unconcerned.

The Phantoms

How did you ever get over being
    terrified?
The shadows, harmless
    but, to your eyes, lurking,
    concealing a presence
    ready to pounce
at any moment,
the leaf gently drifting
    to earth
with no motive,
    startling, as it lands
    on the back of your neck,
the equivocal face you read,
    for no reason,
    in the worst possible way?

How have you survived this long
    with fears
    unsubstantiated,
the clanking sounds of plumbing
gone haywire,
like chained galley slaves
    on a wind tossed frigate,
or the splattered bird
    on your balcony,
    a vague omen
of tragedy swooping in,

and the endless regret
>	you suffered
>	time and again
just to ease your conscience,
>	which it never did,
>	over the offence
>	you mistakenly assumed
you inflicted upon someone
who nonetheless forgave you
>	long ago,
time and again.
>	How did you ever
>	get over the phantoms?
You never did.

Identities

I don't want to be the character
      in the tailored blue suit,
slicked hair, reeking of money
      and advantage,
a trophy woman on his arm,
      as he tosses the keys
to his Cadillac to the valet,
      parts the sea of oglers
jockeying in front of the North
      Italian restaurant for a glimpse,
smoothes down his red silk tie,
      and is shown to his usual
table, but rather the valet, who catches
      the keys, parks and delivers
the cars, calls home to brag
      about the whopping tip
the suit and his girlfriend,
      post-dinner bloated, soused
and wobbly, nonchalantly bestowed
      upon him, and to be happy
simply to mark time until I'm needed.

Resourcefulness

Don't waste time imagining
you could have altered

the course of the blowup
or pretend that clarity will follow.

Don't plead innocence,
make excuses or lay blame

at the nearest doorstep.
Don't fantasize that waking

one minute sooner
would have altered

the outcome, meaning
eternity. All the same, don't

throw up your hands.
Rather, devise strategies

to reassemble your surround,
your self. Salvage the given.

In the aftermath of loss
be grateful you are left.

From smoke and ashes,
fashion hope and play the card

that dares to trump
your destiny—resourcefulness.

one sided

i hate
i hate
i can't hate
anymore
than i hate
that's what comes
of war
i squint
to see
enough
onto collection
plates
i squirt
the blood
i've gathered
from the dead
and wait
for the world
to be
extinguished
it's my fate
that it survives
for i do too little
but hate
too late
and not enough
beyond
i anticipate
annihilation
the more
the better
my sympathy
to the straight
and narrow
who spout
love and peace
i'll not take
a whiff
i'd rather choke
on hate

Split

With each passing
        day, he grows more conscious
of the split—his body, voice,
        movement, thoughts,
distinct, not his own.

He does not analyze
        or critique. He observes,
pulls up loose skin
        from the back of his hand,
and brushes back the hairs

like an animal grooming
        itself. All ears,
he listens to the words
        his mouth forms
but is stymied in knowing how,

or what sparks his love
        for an injured bird
or stirs up tears, and is astonished
        by the routine rise and fall
of his breathing chest.

Most of all, he struggles
        to make sense of which
split self of his it is that wonders
        so, and in which, if any,
his soul resides.

Bozo's Obstacle

I Shall not be Jaded

I may not break out into song
at the sight of the plain-Jane,
under-potted, overwatered
parlor palm on the windowsill,
ignored by the orchid aficionado

proudly showing me the flowering
rarities of his specialty collection,
but my heart is in harmony
with its unobtrusive green modesty
and, under the radar, I blow it a kiss.

Hidden from view, I watch
the old woman as the rain starts,
root for her under my breath,
and nearly intercede as she struggles
to open the rickety umbrella

and finally succeeds after three
failed starts. Silently, I wish
her well as I pass, feeling almost
as if her umbrella is sheltering me
until I sense drops on my neck.

I contemplate the drab sparrow,
having seen its kin countless times
on the same gnarled mulberry tree
that has been in the yard forever,
and with no less amazement

and admiration than if it were
a thousand iridescent peacocks
come out from behind a grove
of banyan fig trees to wander
the grounds of a marble Indian palace.

The Close

Try as I may, to find
an exit, there is no leaving
but through the entrance,

I discover the hard way,
butting my head against
the rock-solid dead end.

The only way out
is through the way in.
Resistant at first to reverse,

at last I take a deep breath,
steel myself, and plunge
headlong through the singular

avenue of escape, exhilarated
by the freedom. I run far,
aimlessly and blind, only

to finally feel and find myself
once more ensnared by another
close, unless it is the same.

All Gone

Pretty much, at least,
gone, whatever you had,

if ever you had it,
in any real way.

Maybe if you scrape
under the sofa, carpet,

floorboards, or dig
in the soil, you'll find

a trace—lint, a chip
of paint, crumbs,

some clue, though it may
not confirm identity

or ownership, and you
could be mistaken

about what it was
you lost or thought,

if anything. It wouldn't be
the first time. A whiff

of remembrance
won't do for proof.

Better to reject
your seeming depletion,

focus on what's left
which is what is,

pick up where you left off
before the needless detour

and quit grieving a loss
as likely hypothetical as not.

The Black Bag

Nothing turned out the way you expected,
so you gave up expecting. You never reacted
the way you intended, so you quit reacting.
You repeatedly failed to see what you wanted
to see so you resolved to keep your eyes closed.
You felt maybe you were on the wrong track,
and there you were on to something. You keep
rummaging through the black bag for the remedy
and discover it's not to be found, probably
was never packed. All the same, the search itself,
shoving aside bottles of tincture, pills, syringes,
plasters, ineffective all, is a consolation because
you tell yourself if you dig deep enough,
long enough, you'll stumble upon a recess,
a secret, zippered compartment, that will hold,
the key to the vault that holds the cure
or, at worst, to another black bag of hope.

No, More than a Stone

I recollect it now,
        for no reason
that I can tell.

I was ten, walking along
        a Sao Paulo street
with my uncle

who thought I bent down
        to retrieve a coin,
and chuckled when, thrilled,

I showed him the brown-
        red stone
streaked with white

like a tiny chunk
        of raw meat
bordered with fat.

He must have thought
        me foolish
to pocket the find.

Over the years, I lost track
        of its whereabouts
more than once

but now and again
        it would surface
unsummoned.

Now, fifty years later,
        when I feel the need
to excavate,

I haven't a clue where
        in the recesses
of my house it may be hiding,

misplaced but never lost.
        I'm sure it will reveal
itself if I give up

the search and put it out
        of my mind, this
ossified meaty nugget

of my tender years, which
        I still see and feel,
and practically taste.

So Far Gone

I can't believe
I can't retrieve
    myself
from this desiccated
    well of loss.

I hesitate to say
I hesitate to try,
    but how
can I deny God's
    honest truth?

Back to the fold
I'd run if I could
    climb out from
my long entrenched
    void.

But it's too much
for me and too much
    to plea
for anyone to ease
    my way.

Perhaps I could enlist
the stars to wield
    their antique light
to help me find
    the route

back to the time
I had a hold on things,
    before I lost
my grip
    and drifted,

to decamp from my rut,
to surface and revamp,
    reuniting
with myself the way
    I was before.

Human Nature

Is it too much to ask
for the vault of bricks
not to topple over me
every morning, and the trip
wire not to be in my path
at night?

I know I have not been
singled out. Misfortune
is indiscriminate. Seek,
though I may, to slip
from its clutches, fate
lies in wait.

One should become
inured. One should
accept with equanimity.
One should not gripe
and insist on shelter
from every storm but,

well, you know—
human nature.

Particulate Matters

Desperately, I strive to set myself
straight but my mind is like vintage

street sweepers, suctionless,
dim-witted mechanical brooms

good at rearranging, not removing,
at best releasing a mist to tamp

down inconvenience, make it
presentable until evaporation

and wind gusts set the world
as astray as ever in a fresh remix.

Repeatedly I swear I'll give up
on misgivings, settle for my God-

given disarray and give in
to the luck of the draw.

Future memories incubating now,
nag at my sanity like a blower

stirring up dust gathered in the folds
of my antiquated cerebral cortex

but it's a relief to be vulnerable.
Uncertainty sweeps over me

with a vengeance, like the line
in the sand I drew inadvertently

as my toe rambled. A fleeting mark
or a bedrock of meaning? I pine

for obliteration and immortality,
seek revelation in the scattering

of ashes (guess whose?) to the four
corners of a world (guess which?).

the illusion of boundaries

not only your own,
      never knowing
      where they stop
or start relative to eternity
but eternity's
      itself, a moment
      in a vaster interval
of meaningless
time better described
      as timeless
      and destined to be
forgotten
were there anyone
      remaining to forget.

not simply your being
      the faintest
      presence
in a borderless world
but that much less
      when stacked up
      against the compass
of worlds in number
unimaginable.
      no great crime
      playing the game
as if distinctions mattered
but don't succumb
      to the folly in fact.

Beliefs

It's a trial for me to shed
commonly held beliefs
at odds with my own.

Too often, I buckle under
to worldly premises divorced
from my clear-as-day truth.

I've seen the tide ebb, and
with it, the shore. Repeatedly,
at that. Doubt all you will.

I peddle what goes around,
a victim of inertia, perhaps
to belong, but at bottom,

am not fooled. My contrary
beliefs trail away like the wake
of a boat, a seagull diminishing

in distance. Bobbing
on the surface, I'm in synch
and alive with the sea's retreat

but dry land tugs back. Doomed
to stand accused of skewed beliefs,
I object even as I tussle

with the mind-numbing
conventional, pressing me to drop
anchor. Willing and able, I'll turn

the tide on these fables yet,
once I summon the courage
to practice what I preach.

The Opposite Horizon

The stars are faint and few but
I, who thrive on recurrent doses
of dark matter, tawdry, unkempt,

where everything is up for grabs,
am in my element. I see well
enough the hidden, the buried,

the not meant to be seen. Daylight,
by comparison, reveals more
than I can tolerate so at its onset

I down a few shots, my cheap
thrill, and sleep through it.
At sun's setting, I search

the opposite horizon for night's
welcome approach, heralded
by the always reliable whistle

of the train heading nowhere,
and I cherish the prospect
of inhabiting the dark

for another spell. Lately,
it takes a good bottle to knock
me out. No complaints there

except for oversleeping
and missing those first dimming
hours. At least the train sounds

right on schedule, waking
me from my stupor and crushing
remnants of the day.

Albeit groggy as all get-out,
I am thankful to be awake,
pointed in the right direction.

The Saving Grace of Turbulence

Overbearing calm and quiet seas
have lulled you into numbness

these many uneventful years.
Then your boat begins to list.

Your breath quickens and life
holds promise again.

The sky darkens with texture,
and questions, long thought

settled, resurface. There is,
renewed, a sense of quest

and urgency, and you must
make decisions or be swallowed.

It is a blessing to be unsettled
by the storm. Air, thin

and turbulent, comes packaged
with salvation. You steer

into the wind, sure to inhale
a bountiful reserve to power

you through future bouts
with tranquility.

Divestiture

I shall return the endless sky,
pensive clouds, distant stars,
the surplus I gathered up

with my too sweeping desire
to have it all. I will loft
the leaves back to their branches,

the trees, back down to earth, for
if I won't uproot myself,
what right have I to look elsewhere?

No more will I horde the birds.
Back to perches, nests, flight
for them all, and let light rebound

to the sun, for I had rather see
than be seen. I retreat to the dark,
relieved to do without. I yield up

my distractions, which took me
too far afield, but won't stop
looking in your eyes, hoping

to retrieve the faint, opalescent
kindness they would reflect
at my urgent stare, when I knew

enough to give more than I took,
and was content with small favors
to uplift my downtrodden heart.

V

Explaining Goldfinches

Only fleetingly would I catch sight of one
but during my usual neighborhood ramble
on the cusp of that particular evening,
they were out in force, synchronized,
uncontained, yellow and black, flitting
from hemlock to spruce, crabapple to yew,
to whatever arboreal cluster of half-bare
branches invited. They'd perch just long
enough for me to get a solid glimpse,
and set my heart to racing as they rose
en masse. At every turn, goldfinches.
I nearly bumped into a neighbor getting out
of his car. I didn't know why he asked
what I was so happy about. Was I smiling?
How could I explain? How could anyone.

The Purple Cress

Ahead of schedule,
except their own,

they stopped me,
sullen, in my tracks,

the modest burst
of purply pink

dotting the ground
beneath the oaks,

too impatient to wait
for spring

but just in time to buoy
my fading spirits.

I returned a meagre
two weeks later,

craving another boost.
Though met by stands

of leafy stems,
their color spent,

that first impression
took root within me deep

enough to prop my droop.
These days, scurrying

on city streets distant
from woodland jaunts

or woods, I call to mind
the purple cress

to keep me on track,
to carry me through.

A Perfect Heart

On the eastern side
of the ancient cherry
tree's trunk, what looks
like a heart skillfully
carved in relief is instead
the close-knit pairing
of a scab with its shadow
cast by morning sun
onto the peeling bark.

The crusty patch itself
could be the remnant
of a thick branch pruned
by a gardener or felled
due to illness, accident,
or age; in sum, the pair
are a heart the tree grew
into, earned, more lifelike
than one could sculpt.

If a passing cloud erases
its outline, it won't have
vanished, only submerged,
and be beating still like
the spirit concealed
in all trees, marking time
until it's revealed in another
of the untold forms
a perfect heart can take.

Smoky Lavender

Say goodbye to rose
and yellow. Cede

the pungent glow
of congenial color

masking the fiction
at its core. Admit

lavender grey
to your heart. Give in

to your birthright
with dusky resolve.

Forfeit the iridescent
rainbow. High time

to open your eyes,
shed the disguise,

embrace the hazy
mauve of truth.

Therein, unadorned,
you'll find your prize.

Mistaken Identities

1.
quiet lamb
on icy meadow?

      no.

silently melting
      block
of snow.

2.
showy yellow flower
among the dogwood's cream?

      not quite.

goldfinch
in a pause
      from flight.

3.
squirrel running zig-zag
to storm drain?

      not at all.

a woman's glove
discarded or lost, windblown,
      primed to fall.

4.
deer about to bolt
from woods?

      no, not.

their spirits
pace in bamboo grove,
      fast caught.

5.
crooning jack-o-lantern
bobbing in the creek?

      no joke

here. floating downstream,
it belts out tunes.
      a melodious bloke.

Pigeons Preening

Hundreds in a corner of the parking
lot at Gravelly Point, where sightseers
congregate to watch jets lift off

from the airport across the river.
They are oblivious to the roaring
fake-winged monsters intruding

on their sky and equally unalarmed
by the grounded people and cars
coming and going, though too close

a threat will see them casually scurry
on the asphalt. Their only concern
is to look charming or, at least, neat.

Once tolerably groomed, they wait
for a lull overhead, their all-clear
signal and, of a sudden, are airborne,

an undulating plane, like a bedspread
fluffed high, a bevy of pigeons
on course to their next landing.

Tree Lesson

To have seen the crabapple
      sapling, planted
deeply and with scrupulous care
      in the recommended
carefully prepared and well-
      drained soil location,
in full sun in April, near dead
      in September despite
consistent watering over
      summer's drought,
10-10-10 fertilization, daily
      inspection, and inordinate
attentiveness throughout,
      and its leaves yellow,
curl, and fall prematurely,
      branches turn brittle,
and snap with the weight
      of a mourning dove,
immune to touted pruning cures
      and gardening nostrums
of every hue and stripe,
      or re-mulching, seen it
on the verge of obliteration,
      and now, in November—
yellow-red crabapples in profusion,
      the tide turned,
and the tree looking more fit
      than ever and ready
for the onslaught of winter, I say,
      "Don't give up on me."

Leaving Marks

Dinosaur footprints,
      bones, teeth, eggs.
Fish and bird fossils.
      Carbon isotopes.

Antelope, hunters—
      ancient cave wall
drawings in charcoal,
      red and green ochre.

Pyramids, terra cotta armies,
      cathedrals, castles,
backyard trellises, arbors,
      long collapsed.

Remains
      of cultivated fields
of fruit, vegetables.
      Something always remains.

Traces of illness,
      scars from wounds,
surgical procedures,
      emotional duress.

Carefully crafted words
      on parchment,
paper, cyberspace, spoken,
      repeated,

misplaced, evaporate
    but not forever.
Crumbs, ghosts
    stubbornly persist.

Minstrel songs, choirs,
    symphonies—still here.
Operas, staged, taped,
    streamed, inescapable.

Excavating, piecing together
    what's left, our calling.
Mosaics, quilts, a pastiche,
    creating, re-creating.

Kiss joined to kiss,
    ring slid on finger—
celebrations. Soldiers, civilians
    falling—commemorations.

Memories remembered,
    restored. Stories
told, retold. The hunger
    not to be forgotten.

About the Author

Originally from New York City, **Phil Wexler** spent his formative years in Brooklyn before moving, as a young man, to Bethesda, Maryland, a suburb of Washington, DC. He has been writing poetry his entire adult life and has had well over 200 poems published in literary magazines. His previous book-length poetry collections include The Sud Parade (prose poems) and The Burning Moustache (both by Adelaide Books), The Lesser Light (Finishing Line Press) With Something Like Hope (Silver Bow Publishing) and I Would be the Purple (Kelsay Books) He has organized and emceed a variety of spoken word reading series' over the years in the Washington, DC area. Passionate about all the arts, Phil also works non-commercially in mosaics. In addition, he collects and tends to his indoor cacti and succulents and, with his wife, Nancy, dotes on their dog, Lucy. Other passions, currently hibernating because there are only so many hours in the day, include bicycling, fencing, and bread-baking.

After a long career of government service as a Technical Information Specialist, Phil retired from the Toxicology and Environmental Health Information Program of the National Library of Medicine, an arm of the National Institutes of

Health. He has edited and authored numerous books and technical journal papers in the field of toxicology. He is Editor-in-Chief of *The Encyclopedia of Toxicology*, 4th edition and *Information Resources in Toxicology*, 5th edition, as well as series editor for a monographic series, *History of Toxicology and Environmental Health*, all published by Elsevier. He is also Editor of *Chemicals, Environment Health: A Global Management Perspective* (CRC Press) and co-Editor-in-Chief of the journal *Global Security: Health, Science and Policy* (Taylor and Francis). A member of the US Society of Toxicology (SOT), he is a recipient of its Public Communications Award and a Trustee of the Toxicology Education Foundation (TEF).

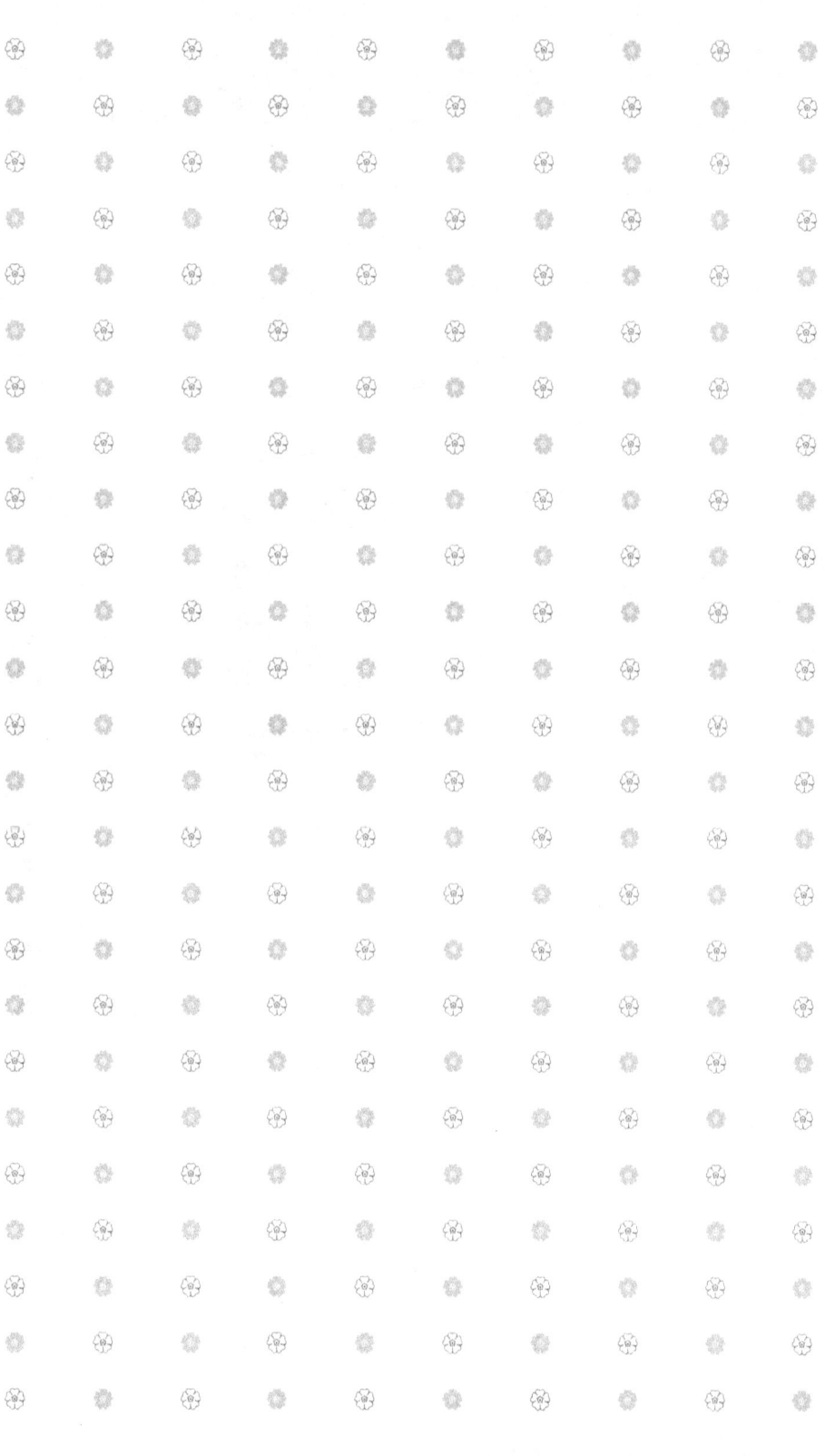

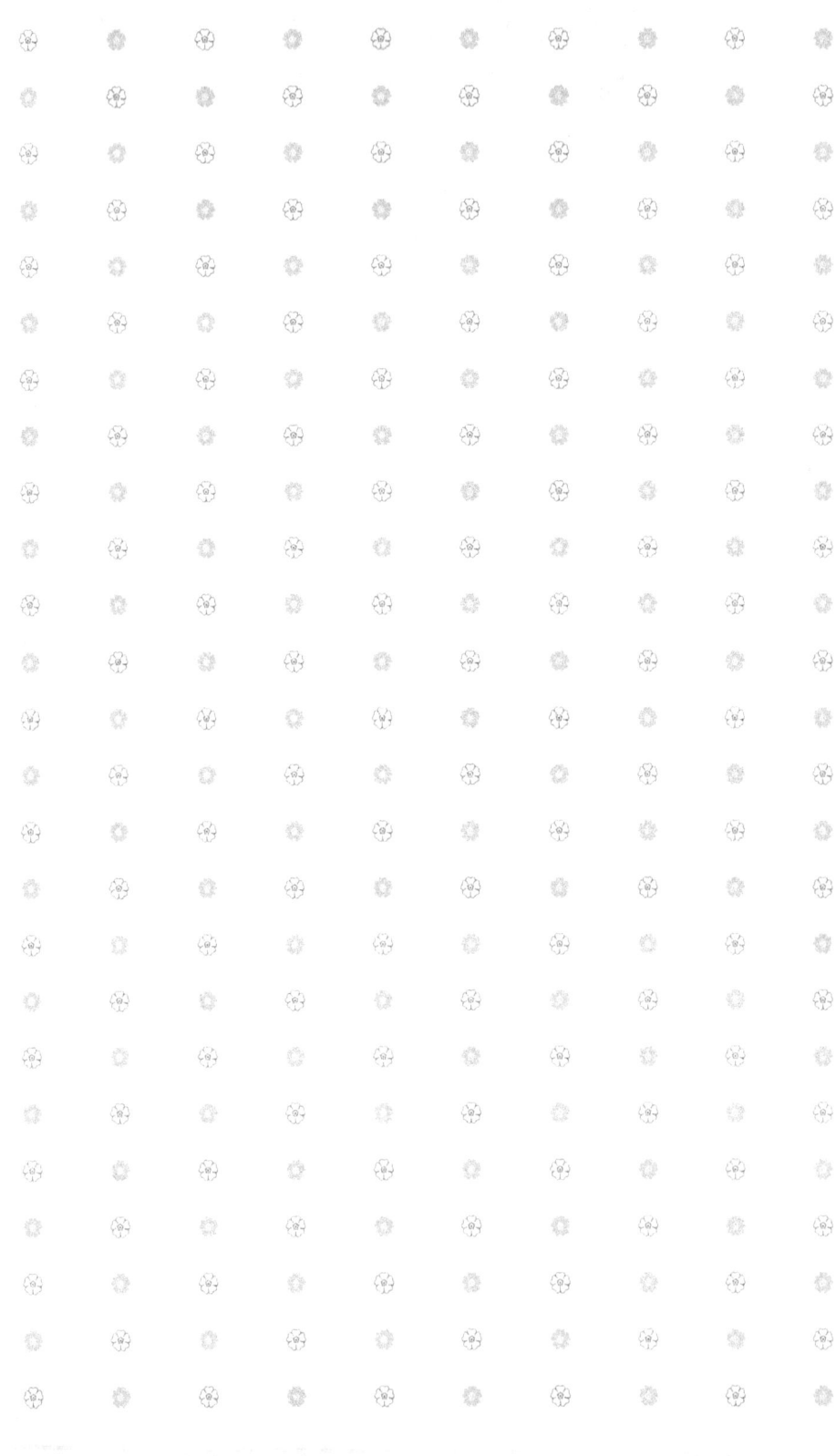

www.ingramcontent.com/pod-product-compliance
Lightning Source LLC
Chambersburg PA
CBHW032337300426
44109CB00041B/1225